Book of Daniel

Memoir Of My Twin Son

THERESE COSIO DELA ROSA

A Book of Daniel by Therese Cosio Dela Rosa

This book is written to provide information and motivation to readers. Its purpose is not to render any type of psychological, legal, or professional advice of any kind. The content is the sole opinion and expression of the author, and not necessarily that of the publisher.

Copyright © 2020 by Therese Cosio Dela Rosa

All rights reserved. No part of this book may be reproduced, transmitted, or distributed in any form by any means, including, but not limited to, recording, photocopying, or taking screenshots of parts of the book, without prior written permission from the author or the publisher. Brief quotations for noncommercial purposes, such as book reviews, permitted by Fair Use of the U.S. Copyright Law, are allowed without written permissions, as long as such quotations do not cause damage to the book's commercial value.

ISBN: 978-1-952822-86-5 (Paperback)
ISBN: 978-1-952822-85-8 (Digital)

Library of Congress Control Number: 2020924309

Printed in Canada and United States of America.

For my beloved Dad & Mom:
HERNANDO GARCIA COSIO
ROSEMARY UHLER COSIO
who, together, are the author of this author.

Chapter 1

EASTER IN HONOLULU

It is April 11, 1971 - Easter Sunday in Honolulu, Hawaii. Very faint slivers of dawn light creep up on the horizon at Honolulu Bay. I am at the operating room of the Tripler Army Medical Center in the hills of Moanalua.

The circular operating theater is throbbing with busy hands of medical personnel hovering over me as I strain in incredible pain. Childbirth is an excruciating experience. This is a **universal** truth…

"C'mon, little mama…you can do it! PUSH!" the attendant nurse wipes my brow as she tries to comfort me. Despite the air-conditioning, sweat embeds my forehead due to the tremendous effort I was straining to expend.

With one supreme thrust, I responded to the "push" command with the most strenuous exertion I could possibly muster. In an instant, I was rewarded with an unexpected calm and absolute silence! My eyes circled around its framework, astounded by a "bird's eye view" of the operating room, meandering over the tops of the heads of surgeons and nurses who were bent intently on a body (**my body???**) sheathed in scattered blankets, with instruments lying on a bed.

Where am I? Who is that person on the bed? Why am I staring down from the ceiling and feeling NO pain? What the heck is happening???

I was astonished beyond words…Years later, after having schooled myself on "other-worldly" literature, I would recognize this as an "out-of-body experience." At that moment, it was totally new to me.

However, it was very pleasant, as all the pain no longer existed and I felt at peace. But the voices continued to beckon to me…

"Are you all right, little mama? C'mon, little mama… please be okay!" faintly echoed as soft hands patted my face and hair. When I finally moaned, the surgeon stated with great relief: "Baby A is 4 lbs. 11 oz. and is a male"…handing the infant over to a pediatrician who patted the baby dry, cutting its umbilical cord and placing him in an incubator.

Seven minutes later, after skillfully maneuvering the position of Baby B as far removed from its breech stance as possible and using the appropriate forceps, the second infant was born at 5 lbs. 15 oz. and placed in a separate incubator.

The alertness and remarkable preparation of the medical personnel and Operating Room staff was unusual. The fact is, they had been pre-conditioned by a similar incident a few days earlier, at which a twin birth had resulted in the death of one of the babies (due to comparable circumstances). It was like experiencing an actual fire incident right after having gone through a fire drill in the same location. Whether this was a happenstance, or an "act of God" is subject to interpretation.

At any rate, this Easter birth was the day Baby A (Daniel) made his entrance on this earth. It seemed as though he couldn't wait to come into this world! Earlier (during the "labor" phase), he and his brother had caused extreme concern among the staff because the bigger baby B (Gabriel) was pressing down hard upon the smaller baby A (Daniel) to the point at which the doctors feared that baby A would suffocate…They had to summon the head surgeon to the hospital while they prepped me to undergo a Cesarian section by marking my abdomen with "x" signs where I would be cut open!

I prayed harder than I had ever done that it would not come to that, when the head surgeon finally arrived and they managed to maneuver baby A (Daniel) away from sure death…

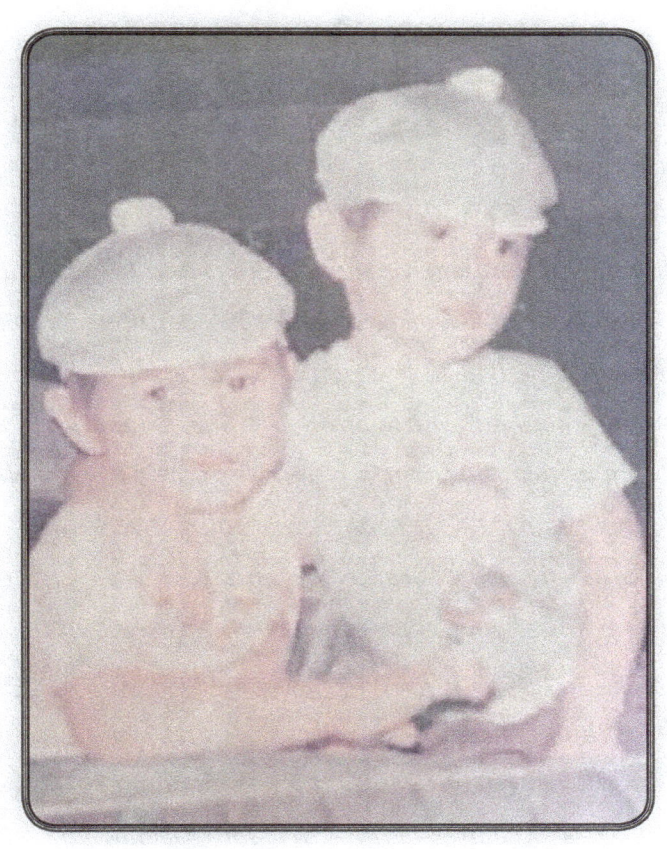

BABY DANIEL & BABY GABRIEL

AFTERTHOUGHT

Hindsight, as we all know, is 20/20. Years later, as I ponder on the birth order of my twin sons, it occurs to me how "short" Daniel's lifetime was meant to be, having died at the tender age of 34.

As a consequence, I wonder whether, in some preternatural way, Daniel was conscious that he did not have very long to live, and therefore, he was driven!!!

He was in a hurry to come out into this world! He came out first and eagerly because he knew he had to live hard and fast…

Later, during the short course of his lifetime, he repeatedly compacted his activities in order to achieve maximum results as quickly as possible. For example, he held down 3 separate part-time jobs in the summer to be able to buy his first airplane that he could fly when weather permitted. This, instead of dating girls or wallowing in drugs/alcohol or other vices. But he always had the time to feed the wild birds or strum his guitar or pound his drums or learn to play the piano and the violin during troubled nights.

Throughout his length of days, Daniel operated on the assumption that he constantly needed to shoot a three-pointer in a split second, but not at the expense of love for family or nature!

Chapter 2

AT HOME IN HONOLULU

It was a fitful night after the childbirth that I spent in the recovery room. Due to the extensive trauma of the birthing experience, I suffered a couple of instances of excessive bleeding before the staff could release me to a regular room.

The next morning, I was pleasantly surprised when my husband and 18-month old daughter Lara came to visit with my mom and dad (who had flown in from New Jersey). It was delightful to share my twin sons' birth with my parents and family

We were catching up on the latest clan news when an attendant quietly came over and placed an armful of clean folded sheets onto the foot of my bed. Seeing this, my mom (who never fails to speak her mind) made ready to get up and move away in anticipation that the attendant would make up the bed with fresh sheets.

As an aside, my mother is a half-American Filipino wife who had given birth to nine babies in the Philippines, during the course of which she accumulated a rich experience of hospital birthing practices. Without exception, in those days, childbirth in a Philippine hospital involved the attendants always changing the bedsheets. At the same time, the new mother is pampered hand and foot with total service and care in the hospital during the first weeks of childbirth.

Thus, we were all shocked when the attendant stated matter-of-factly, "Oh, I'm not changing the sheets… The fresh sheets are all here and ready, but the patient is expected to do the job herself…"

My mom: "Are you kidding me??? She just had twin babies last night and suffered extensive hemorrhage afterwards…You are changing the sheets, not my daughter!" At which the frightened attendant proceeded to assist me onto the adjoining empty bed while she changed the sheets.

That was emblematic of how my parents had always overprotected me and my siblings all our lives. In order to ease my first weeks at home, they decided to stay with us in Honolulu despite the fact that my mom was on leave from work and my dad had just started a business.

Meanwhile, my dad had set in motion the paper trail that would enable his mother (my grandmother) to come from the Philippines and stay with me in Honolulu to help care for the 3 babies while my husband (a Navy submarine Supply CPO) fulfilled his sea duty.

Needless to say, the physical work involved in caring for 3 babies is very taxing. We had our daughter Lara (18 months old at the time) and the twins Daniel and Gabriel Jr. To top it all, my husband does not cook but is very picky about food (he does not eat leftovers). And since my childbirth was two months premature, we had had nothing done in preparation for it at all.

In fact, since it was Easter weekend, we had gone to the Ala Moana shopping mall in Honolulu to buy an Easter basket for Lara. I was very heavy with child and could hardly walk, so I spent most of the time sitting on the mall benches while waiting for Lara and her dad to roam around the mall.

Next morning, Easter Saturday, my husband was scheduled for guard duty aboard ship at the yard; and would have to stay there overnight. I started the day doing mounds of laundry; but was very bothered that I kept wetting my underpants. Although I had previously given birth (to Lara), I was quite uninformed (or had forgotten) about "breaking water." My first child birthing experience had as a precursor a spotting of blood—**not** water. So that's what my psyche focused on as a harbinger to childbirth (not breaking water)…

So, I called my husband on the ship to report what was happening. He was the one who insisted that I call the hospital to find out what I should do. When I called, the nurse insisted that I come to the hospital straightaway, since I was about to give birth!

Two months before my due date! (Not unusual with multiple births, according to the nurse.) But being so unprepared, I tried to reason with the nurse that was long before my due date; however, she firmly insisted that it was time for me to go to the hospital. After I called my husband to relay the message, he received his XO's approval to go home.

Lara and I were all set and ready to go (even though I had **not** had the time to shower and wash my hair); with luggage all packed…But when my husband arrived, he **insisted** that he needed to shower and change! You would think he was the one who was about to give birth!

The husband's degree of self-importance is absolutely inflated by virtue of expecting a child—let alone twins! When my husband returned to work after the twins were born, he exultantly informed me that there was a long line of personnel queued up outside his office door, waiting to congratulate him on the birth of our twin sons! Oh, well…what I would have given to have him endure one iota of my labor pains…

AFTERTHOUGHT

Parents come in all shapes and sizes! Mine were seasoned (after 9 children) while my husband and I were "neophytes" in comparison.

Men are more excitable/nervous/perturbed… while women are more serene, with a greater capacity to stay calm (at least in our case). Of course, this is not true in all instances (allowing for sharp differences in emotional/psychological temperaments). For example, my mom and dad were the opposite case—my dad was always the calm one, while my mom was often a nervous wreck.

I believe it all depends on a person's threshold for physical pain—the higher it is, the better able one is to control one's nervous system. This is not a scientific pronouncement but an experiential assertion. Our children will often mirror one or both of our parents' attitudes and/or mannerisms. It becomes more visible as time passes…

When parents have more than one child, each is a unique individual with varying talents and weaknesses (often mirroring one or both parents, grandparents, or other relatives). This often leads a parent to feel closer to the child who is most akin to him/her. Or an aunt/uncle will exhibit a special affinity to the child who most resembles them physically or who manifests a particular gift, e.g. music.

This has fueled the recent popularity of inquiries into ancestry and genetic histories. Somehow, a person feels more anchored in his/her personal situation when founded on solid, historical grounds!

Chapter 3

ODYSSEY WITH LOLA OYENG

Her name was "Dolores." She was my grandmother (my Dad's mom) who arrived in Honolulu from the Philippines to help me with my 3 babies. At age 63, she was still hale and hearty (besides being a marvelous cook). I certainly welcomed her assistance after my parents had gone back to their busy lives in New Jersey.

Our days were filled with dirty diapers ("Pampers" had not yet arrived on the scene); laundry; sterilizing 36 baby bottles (in between nursing the twins at each of my breasts as I held one at each arm while sitting on a rocking chair); while feeding a toddler; cleaning house; hanging wet laundry on the clothesline; etc.etc.etc! No wonder the days sped by like a blur…

My husband had proceeded with his sea duty routine and his nuclear submarine regularly went out to sea on patrol of the Tonkin Gulf during the height of the Vietnam War. Besides the regular patrols, they would go out on weekly sea trials testing new equipment. So, he was gone approximately 6 to 9 months of each year away at sea! As a result, my grandmother and I were left at home to do housework and child-rearing much of that time.

Technically, she was "great" grandmother to my kids; but in the Philippines, we have a sort of "universal" title that is used to address grandparents, i.e. "Lolo" and "Lola."

One legacy of the country's long colonialism by Spain is the adoption of numerous Hispanic words and phrases into the Filipino language. Hence, the Spanish terms "aguelo" and "aguela" for "grandfather/ grandmother" became corrupted into "Lolo" and "Lola." and my grandmother's given name "Dolores" evolved into her nickname "Loleng" which further metastasized into "Oyeng." Thus, she became "Lola Oyeng."

Elderly relatives in the Philippines have an unsavory practice of forming "favorites" among children and grandchildren. Lola Oyeng was no exception. Her attitude towards Lara, my eldest child, seemed naturally combative because the little girl, being the first child, assumed a supervisory role over her baby brothers. The boys, on the other hand, resumed their tight relationship in the womb by remaining exclusively wrapped up in intimate attention to each other.

So close was the boys' relationship that they actually developed their own "private" dialect by which they communicated with each other. None of us understood what was being said to the other, except for the two of them. It was astonishingly obvious by their reactions to each other that they profoundly enjoyed their "dialogues."

Lola Oyeng figured that she would be partial to the twin Gabriel Jr. since he is the namesake of his father (a birth position considered **special** in Filipino culture). She was also a very social person and had made friends with another Filipino family who lived 4 houses away from us. Because I was still in the process of trying to obtain my driver's license, Lola Oyeng prevailed upon her friend Norma to come with me for practice drives around our subdivision. Thanks to her help, in addition to my teary-eyed pleas to the DMV officer, I finally obtained my driver's license after **5 failures**! (To this day, I purposely **avoid** parallel-parking...)

The twins' baptismal party was also a success due largely to Lola Oyeng's expertise in preparing fancy Filipino foods. All of the guests were my husband's Filipino friends and family members.

Unfortunately, conflict arose between me and Lola Oyeng, who continued to practice her favoritism. I found that such behavior would ultimately result in damaged psyches among my tender kids. At the same time, my siblings in New Jersey developed a need for child care for their own growing broods. And so ended our odyssey with Lola Oyeng, when she traveled to New Jersey to help the rest of the family.

LARA AND BROTHERS IN HONOLULU

AFTERTHOUGHTS

Family generations play a significant role in the genesis of individual personalities. There is a give-and-take relationship between older and younger generations (usually a "see-saw" process).

Sometimes it takes years; or an instantaneous hindsight that comes with unexpected trauma or tragedy. A tremendous jolt to a person's psyche will often precipitate a guilty pang that one could have (**should have???**) treated an older relative with greater kindness. Wisdom **does** come with age, along with time and space.

In the moment, an adult is governed by gut instincts as well as learned social/cultural mores. There is an uncomfortable juxtaposition of shame and honor in the painful flowering of a person's character. It is often a slow and cumbersome process. But the ultimate realization will shake one to her core to become a heart rending memorable moment…

Apres mois les deluge…

Chapter 4

Cross-country road trip

We were a "nuclear" family again: mother, father, daughter and sons! And, happily, my husband came to the end of his 4-year sea duty. We would return to shore duty on the mainland! However, his next duty station was to the Portsmouth Naval Shipyard in Kittery, Maine. What a change! From the swaying palms of Honolulu to the winter wonderlands of New England…

We decided to take advantage of the geography by shipping our car to San Francisco; placing our household goods in storage; driving from California across the country to the opposite coast of Maine. It would be our next adventure! We would visit with family and friends along the way!

Our first stop was San Francisco, where we stayed with the Limjocos, close family friends; as well as with my Auntie Ida who lived close to the Disney theme park. Of course, we took the kids to Disneyland, which was very hectic but enjoyable. It barely mattered that I was also 3 months pregnant with our 4th child, and not exactly in tip-top shape.

Also, the boys were in the late stages of toilet training; while Lara resumed her "big sister" role. Bathroom became a major issue during our times on the road. We often frequented a Holiday Inn to rest and use the facilities. It became so ubiquitous that, whenever anybody expressed the need to go "pee," the boys would cheerily chime in, "Daddy, why don't you just buy a Holiday Inn?" Ha, ha, ha…we giddily responded!

At Disney World, Lara was fascinated by the Cinderella castle with its footmen and daintily dressed ladies in-waiting. And we couldn't help singing along as we rode the circulating cab cars to the tune of "It's a small world after all…"

The boys swooned over the little racing cars, the twirling miniature airplanes, and the inimitable roller coaster! Our breaths were literally taken away with every heart-thumping ride. By the time we settled back into my aunt's house, we were totally wound up!

In Chicago, we stayed at my husband's brother's place near the hospital where he worked as a surgeon. His wife was a Registered Nurse and they had 3 children (2 girls and a boy). The cousins haltingly interacted with one another. They accompanied our family to see the tourist sites in the state.

Chicago has grown more than a hundredfold from a small trading post at the mouth of the Chicago River into one of the country's largest cities. It has experienced rapid growth into a global city, a place where people of every ethnicity have come to pursue the "American dream."

We visited Fort Dearborn at the corner of Michigan Avenue and Wacker Drive. The city has become a hub of trading possibilities, fueled by 50% of the rail freight that continues to pass through Chicago. It has also become one of the nation's busiest aviation centers, thanks to O'Hare and Midway airports.

After the Great Chicago Fire of 1871, the city rebuilt quickly. Waves of immigrants came to take jobs in the factories and meatpacking plants. The first skyscraper, a 10-story steel-framed Home Insurance Building, was built in 1884 at LaSalle and Adams streets and demolished in 1931.

Finally, we took the opportunity to climb to the top of the 1,450-foot Sears Tower, completed in 1974, which at the time was the tallest building in North America and the 3rd tallest in the world.

We continued our trip through Arizona where we marveled at the "Painted Desert." The desert is roughly 120 miles long by 60 miles wide, bordered by the Mogollon Plateau, the Mogollon Rim, and the Arizona transition zone. It is composed of stratified layers of easily erodible siltstone, mudstone, and shale. The fine grained layers contain lots of iron and manganese compounds which provide the pigments of brilliant and varied colors; not only gray and red colored bands across the landform, but even shades of lavender.

At an early age, the twins had manifested a fascination with ornate shapes and colors of various hues. The sight of the Painted Desert awakened the "artist' instinct in them. They were in complete awe and took everything in with deep and silent amazement

We warily skirted tornado warnings as we drove throughout the plains. We climbed around the twisted mountainous pathways of Utah, with stops at the Grand Canyon.

Located in southwestern Utah, the Bryce Canyon National Park is literally not a canyon. It is actually a group of giant natural amphitheaters and geological structures called "hoodoos," or pinnacles. The site is a geologist's dream, with its orange, red and white coloring of rocks that together comprise a spectacular view. Numerous visitors arrive at the canyon to hike, camp, stargaze, and otherwise drink in the stunning vistas.

We were mesmerized by the immense panorama of cliffs and rocks and inundating crevices and ragged crags and valleys. It was a sight to behold—a penetrating feast for our eyes and souls! The experience sustained our spirits for the rest of our trip to Virginia.

Arriving in Virginia, we visited my younger sister Angela and her husband Rey who lived in Richmond with their daughters whom we had never met until then. It was a blissful reunion.

My sister and brother-in-law took us on a classic trolley ride around Richmond, during which we saw the site where Patrick Henry delivered his famous influential speech. Other sites included edifices that date back to the Civil war; as well as statues of confederate generals along Monument Avenue.

We passed through the glittering banks of the James River, as we sat aboard a lovingly restored trolley with its bright red paint and intricately wooden seats. We went past the Hollywood Cemetery to explore stories of presidents, Supreme Court Justices, and prominent Richmond families. We learned about Presidents Jefferson David and John Tyler; as well as the scandalous Richmond banker who survived the sinking of the Titanic!

All in all, it was a historic visit to one of the first settlements in the country. We were satiated with the aura of history!

Our next stop was New Jersey, where the rest of my family lived. There were my Mom and Dad; older sister Claire and her family; two younger brothers Don and Mon; younger sister Cora; (our youngest sister Malou had just been married and lived in the Philippines with her husband.) So, our family was "quasi" complete.

In the early 1960's, members of my extended family first settled in the small town of Elizabeth, New Jersey. Originally called "Elizabethtown" it was founded in 1664 by English settlers; but not named for Queen Elizabeth. In fact, it was named for Elizabeth, wife of Sir George Carteret, one of the two original Proprietors of the colony of New Jersey. The town served as the first capital of New Jersey.

Eventually, members of my family scattered among neighboring towns, including Piscataway, which is the fifth oldest municipality in N.J. Piscataway has grown from an Indian territory, through a colonial period; and is one of the links in the earliest settlement of the Atlantic seacoast.

It is in Piscataway's Resurrection Cemetery where the departed members of my own family have been interred. It is there where my son Daniel's final resting place is located, along with my parents, sister, brother-in-law, and niece. It is where we always go to pay our love and respect.

Everyone was charmed by Lara and the twins, especially the twins who were a "first" in the family. Our children were engulfed with love and attention by our newfound extended family.

It was a prelude to future reunions for significant events like birthdays, baptisms, confirmations, weddings, anniversaries, and (sadly) funerals. But at least this time there was no longer a big, blue ocean separating our own nuclear family from its cosmic cohort. We would always be connected in heart and in spirit!

MOTHER AND KIDS

AFTERTHOUGHT

Geography is a remarkable factor in family relationships. It separates parents from children, siblings from each other, cousins, aunts, uncles, grandparents, etc. Keeping track can become a shield or a weapon.

Circumstances that precipitate separation are often planned but usually unexpected. Children can choose to gravitate towards areas where they can work and/or live sustainably. Weather conditions are often a factor, especially as people age and/or become invalid. Romantic relationships can be a determinant. Whatever the lynchpin is, a person's character will often determine whether time and/or distance will play a role to either further or obliterate relationships.

Strength of will can be a catalyst. Sometimes, the universe will intercede to allow a happy intervention. Other times, the best-laid plans can be extinguished by unalterable karma…

Que sera, sera!

Chapter 5

SCHOOL DAYS IN KITTERY, MAINE

After the wide Hawaiian expanse of big, blue skies dotted with swaying palm trees and lengths of panoramic white-sand beaches, it was a welcome change to insert oneself into the compact, steady New England village atmosphere of the Town of Kittery, Maine. With its snappy cold breezes, quaint antiques, and salty air swirling around stately Cape Cod style mansions and lighthouses, Kittery is a sight to behold!

My pregnancy was a burden in the process of moving into our ranch-style military housing accommodations. Because of the size of our family, we occupied an entire duplex (ordinarily available to two single-family units) bordering upon a creek that extended out onto mudflats. Eventually, my husband acquired a second hand boat on which he would take the boys fishing; as well as conduct the family and visitors on boat rides across the Piscataqua River.

In the meantime, the boys were immersed in their educational process, attending the local public schools. Lara was in first grade, while the boys tackled kindergarten.

Early on, the boys exhibited unusual artistic skills and showed proclivities for drawing detailed sailing ships. Gabriel Jr. won 1st prize with his portrayal of a Christmas scene during a town-wide contest. And when I came to pick them up one afternoon, the elementary principal made a point of meeting with me. After our introductions, she invited me to her office to show me an intricate drawing of a sailing ship with all its sails unfurled. It was magnificent! And she proudly declared it was the work of my boys! I literally burst with pride!

Throughout their early elementary grades (and onto high school and college), the twins excelled in math and music, as well as exhibiting an expansive literary background (which had actually caught me unawares).

Every year, I inevitably attended those ubiquitous parent-teacher conferences with my children's teachers. As a consequence of my own graduate school education in Comparative Literature, I had accumulated my own little library of many literary works—from early tales like Beowulf and Chaucer's Canterbury Tales, to Shakespeare and the Romantic/Metaphysical Poets, etc. Unbeknownst to me, my twins had been helping themselves during their spare time to reading the books in my own library, to their own delight! As such, when I had the occasion to confer with their third grade teacher, he made it a point to complement me on the reading prowess of my twins. He related how, on one occasion, he had served as a monitor during the class' "study period" and he came upon my boys in an animated dialogue about the characters in Beowulf! Astonished, the teacher questioned them further about the plot and characters; and was amazed at their insights and analyses! I was speechless as he continued to complement me on my sons' unusual evidence of advanced literary acumen!

On another occasion (also at a parent-teacher conference), I was stopped in the hallway on my way to confer with a math teacher. The lady who confronted me identified herself as the Art teacher, and she asked me if my boys had had art lessons. I smiled and said "No." She promptly stated that, in all her years of teaching art, she had never encountered kids may sons' age who could draw so well! She marveled at their innate artistic talent and urged me to help them develop their skills. She proceeded to show me evidence of their talent.

Besides their startling educational development, the twins and Lara also grew in faith and spirit. All three of them received First Communion at St. Raphael's Church in Kittery, to which parish we belonged. Of course, they had completed the required catechetical instructions, coupled with our regular attendance in church services. We also strove to teach them by our example.

All three children were innately shy and reserved in character; although they could be rambunctious at play. Lara was always motherly and protective with her brothers; and the boys inevitably avoided any instances of disappointing me. However, Danny was not averse to stretching the limits of my patience (mostly because he knew I could **never** bear to hurt him). He instinctively knew we had a bond between us that was always there.

Somehow I felt a little guilty that it seemed that I treated Danny with greater attention than his siblings. But it was because he was the **frail** one (having been born with a heart murmur which had made him stay longer in the incubator at the hospital); apart from the fact that he was the smaller in size.

Another factor that became evident as they matured was the fact that Danny exhibited what's called a "lazy eye." All that it means is that one of the muscles inside one of his eyeballs was weaker (and a little bit longer) than the other ones, tending to delay its reaching its focal point instantaneously. According to the ophthalmologist, Dan needed surgery to excise part of the muscle and shorten it enough to speed up its focusing.

We took Danny to the Portsmouth Hospital where I stayed with him overnight for the surgery. He came through successfully; and we were back safely with the family.

The children took up in school where they had left off, after the hospital stay. Family life continued serenely…

LARA & BROTHERS & SISTER IN KITTERY

AFTERTHOUGHT

When children are left to their own resources, surprise happens. Innate characteristics sprout as nurtured by environmental (as well as genetic) factors such as exposure to books, colors, instruments, natural wonders and objects like rainbows, white caps on ocean waves, sunrises and sunsets, tweeting of birds, symphonies, sad songs, etc.

We need to indulge our fellow travelers on life's journey with examples of courage; as well as of humility, empathy, and patience. A smile is always a welcome form of greeting to strangers.

Education is paramount but must sometimes take second place to experience. There is nothing more real than being in the moment. We must revere the sacrament of the moment—the "now." Yesterday is done and gone. Tomorrow may never come. Our only true reality is NOW… Let us live it to the fullest!

Vision is both interior and exterior. Sometimes a physical hindrance becomes an asset when the spirit intervenes to facilitate the desired experience. It often enables the handicapped individual to accomplish super-human feats! Let us never underestimate those who have physical handicaps…

Chapter 6

Junior High School Through College

When the boys were four years old, we welcomed the birth of our second daughter, Charmaine Marie. She was a precocious child, having learned to recite the pledge of allegiance at 18 months of age (after regular exposure to Sesame Street and Mister Rogers). Her twin brothers became eager mentors who welcomed her into their own little "book club" at my library; and finely honed her reading skills. She became a skilled reader at the tender age of 2!

Every Sunday at church, adults who sat near us were amazed at how adept this little girl was in following the biblical readings during mass. Everyone expressed disbelief at discovering she was only 2 years old!

The primary disadvantage was her birthdate, December 19, which made her ineligible to enroll in kindergarten before her fifth birthday. I appealed it to the School Superintendent, who invited us to her office so that she could be tested as to her aptitudes. After the testing, they concluded that her aptitudes actually placed her at the third grade level at age 5. As a concession, they agreed to accept her into the first grade at age 5 without going through kindergarten (even though she was already at third grade level). From that point on, she was so advanced that she always made the honor roll all through school.

The twins were likewise on the honor roll throughout school. In fact, they both graduated in the "Top Ten" of their high school class. They were also active on the Math Club; Jazz Club; Concert Band; and the Marching Band.

Dan's musical talent became apparent when he mastered playing the drums without a single lesson! He also taught himself to play the piano and the guitar (and later on, the violin)!

We took him to neighboring schools to participate in the Marching Band competitions. He performed in concerts at school with the Jazz Band and the Concert Band. His brother Gabe received standing ovations during guitar performances by the Jazz Band.

On Christmas, when I asked him what he wanted as a gift, he stated that he wanted a violin. When I protested that he didn't know how to play the violin, he replied that he could teach himself just like he had done with the drums, the guitar, and the piano. **And so he did!**

His twin brother Gabe was equally musical in that he took a few basic guitar lessons but developed them on his own. He enjoyed standing ovations during concerts; but was always terrified of public appearances. His shyness was so ingrained in him that he actually deliberately misspelled a word during a spelling bee contest when he realized that all the other contestants would be eliminated and he could be the only one remaining in front of a huge audience. To avoid that awful reality, he preferred to disqualify himself deliberately!

Between the two brothers, Dan took the "leader" Alpha male position (perhaps because he was actually the firstborn???) in everyday activities. Dan was usually the first to respond verbally in conversations; and in school he was the one who initially made friends. Gabe basically "shadowed" his brother and "adopted" his friends.

During their first year in college, they started as "entrance scholars" by virtue of their graduation in the Top Ten of their High School class. Both decided to major in Music; but only Dan joined the Concert Band. We had him fitted with the required tux and cummerband.

They lived in the school dormitory during weekdays and came home on weekends so they could hold down part-time jobs. Since I was working for the Town of Wells at the time, I managed to get them jobs at the Town's local business establishments.

We also continued to spend holidays in New Jersey with the rest of the family. Christmas was always a special time when my brothers and sisters arrived from various states (California, Virginia, Maine) to congregate at my eldest sister's house in New Jersey.

It was customary for the family to hold a musical festival Christmas when various members displayed their musical talents. Grandkids would sing and/or play musical instruments. Aunts and uncles and cousins would do the same. It became a family tradition led by my father, who voiced a beautiful tenor! The COSIOs would become a family of music!

Around the same time, my husband furthered his interest in piloting airplanes; and encouraged our boys to take it up by paying for their flying lessons. Danny loved the experience; to the point where he wanted to have his own airplane; and built one (with the help of his brother) from a model plane kit. This was right after he had passed the practical pilot test with "flying" colors and obtained his very own pilot's license.

Continually in a "driven" mode, Danny worked 3 part-time jobs on weekends just so he could afford to buy a 2-seater Cessna which he piloted on weekends (whenever weather permitted).

It is one of my deepest heartaches that I never said "yes" whenever my dear, sweet Dan asked me to go fly with him…It was particularly regretful that I never got to experience the fantastic foliage sight of a New England autumn with him! Dan described it in superlative terms and he always extolled the experience of flying! THIS REMAINS THE ONE EVERLASTING PAIN I WILL BEAR…

DAN'S PLANE WITH FAMILY

AFTERTHOUGHTS

The truth lies in our genes and chromosomes. The person that we become has been proscribed at the moment of our conception, at a cellular level. Our experiences shade and color that personality to various degrees, depending on the concomitant emotions involved.

Our lives intersect with other lives which summarily affect our actions and reactions. Often, the path on which we choose to walk is conditioned by extraneous circumstances (as well as innate emotional and intellectual ones). Sometimes we are influenced by a person whom we deeply admire; or by one of our own family members; or simply by our ancestry.

Aspiration of dreams is always a personal goal. Every person has a dream (whether expressed or not). The thread of life is loosened by our actions and interactions, in response to, or to incite specific events. Our ambitions will be met eventually by either triumph or defeat. Much depends on the strength of our dreams…

A dream is "a wish the heart makes" (as the song goes)…when we're fast asleep. Sleep is a potent factor in our lives. It has been said that the last idea or final thought in your mind just before falling asleep governs what is dreamt. Who knows what is ingrained in one's mind at any given point? It could be a totally subconscious thought!

Inevitably, "che sera…sera…"

Chapter 7

AFTER COLLEGE

Both young men spent busy days studying on weekdays and working on weekends. Dan exhibited his profound love of nature through his devotion to the local bird population. He built little bird houses which he situated around the numerous trees surrounding our house.

When my brother-in-law cleared a portion of our backyard to allow the swimming pool to obtain maximum sunlight, both Dan and Gabe angrily objected to the cutting of the trees. They demanded that I tell my brother in-law to put down his chain saw and leave the trees be!!! I tried to reason with them that the water in the pool needed to get warmed up by the sun; but there was too much shade because of the trees; so my brother-in-law was just "thinning" that portion of our three acres. They grudgingly accepted my explanation.

However, it did not stop Dan from hanging bird feeders around the house; and with his own money, spent a lot of it on bags of birdseed and other foods which he distributed among them (even amid feets of snow in the wintertime).

In fact, he bought books and videotapes about birds and could identify the various breeds. He loved showing me the differences between mourning doves and cardinals, etc. etc. He even asked me to plant bright red flowers near his bedroom window, to attract hummingbirds.

I remember a particular instance when he kept calling out to me: "Mom…mom… hurry up and see…" There was a hummingbird making a buzzing sound, rapidly flitting its wings just outside his bedroom window! We shared that precious moment that I now treasure!

As a matter of fact, after his death, when we went to Dan's office to empty his desk of his personal belongings, there was a drawer filled with parts of bird feeders. His office mates explained that, indeed, Dan had set up bird feeders on a few trees that surrounded their office building! Dan's love of nature was unimpeded!

His brother Gabe had gotten a job offer in New Hampshire, our neighboring state; and decided to assert his independence by renting his own apartment close to his job site. Both brothers had earned bachelor's degrees in Computer Science (a field of employment that was quite in demand at the time). But since Gabe had been living on his own quarters, we only saw him occasionally.

Dan, on the other hand, received a job offer in Falmouth, Maine; and chose to live at home (so he could fly his plane on weekends). At that time, his second-hand car was on its last legs; and since he had just landed a good job with a hefty salary, he decided to buy himself a brand new car!

It was quite an experience when he asked me to accompany him to a car dealer so he could make the purchase. Since we already had a Subaru SUV, which gave us excellent performance, we agreed to go to the Subaru dealership where we had purchased our car. Dan chose a beautiful blue-green Subaru Impreza to test drive; and after some discussions and haggling, signed a sales agreement. He drove home in his brand new car; and we were both pleased with his choice. Because his office would be a little distance away from our home, he acquired an "EZ Pass" toll-paying machine. And whenever his car was scheduled for oil change/checkup, we would switch cars so that I could take his car to the dealer for regular maintenance. It continued a beautiful mother-son relationship that had started from his infancy.

Today, as I look back to the time when Dan lived with us, I feel a deep sense of gratitude for the time we had spent together. Every day, I would wait to hear the hum of his car pulling into the driveway. He would often keep me company in the kitchen while I cooked dinner; and we would discuss anything and everything (from current news, to political figures, to the latest family events.) I consider it a gift from God that He allowed this close bonding with a son whom I had no idea I would be losing soon!

And his love for music continued. We have an old piano at home, which Dan taught himself to play. He also had his drums from his Marching Band stint in high school, which he often played (and brought the house down during local competitions). His musical prowess extended to teaching himself to play the guitar. On many evenings (after dinner) I would hear him strumming melancholy tunes on his guitar; and my heart ached with him and for him…

Dan continued to fly his plane whenever the weather allowed. He never failed to invite me along; but my dominant fear was always an imaginary newspaper headline: "Mother and son lost in plane crash!" In my mind, I decided I would eventually fly with him in his plane just as my husband, youngest daughter, and Gabe Jr. had done…

It has become particularly haunting in the fall, when the legendary colors of autumn in New England states summon so-called "leaf peepers" from surrounding states (and other countries) flock to Maine. Dan always proclaimed how fantastic the scenery is from up in the air! Too bad I never took him up on it! **That plane was the love of Dan's life…**

AFTERTHOUGHT

Regret is a pain-filled human emotion, filled with "woulda" and "shoulda" statements. No human being is exempt from it, from the standpoint that we are all imperfect.

We only sometimes know what to do and when to do it. Mostly, we stumble and make mistakes! Circumstances and time constraints often stand in our way. Unfortunately, it is only later on when we come to the realization that things could have turned out differently (and usually more happily)… That is the tragedy of regret…

Proximity is a gift that promotes loving relationships. It allows interactions up close and personal, which only serve to heighten the activity of endorphins in our brains; thus leading to explosions of "good," warm feelings. This is one of the reasons why hugs are so precious; and why babies are said to not be able to survive without human touch!

I like to believe that there is a power much higher than us who is also most wise, in allowing us the time and space to experience physical closeness at its maximum when a lifetime is due to be cut short…

DANIEL AFTER COLLEGE

Chapter 8

MOVE TO NEW JERSEY

The computer or "Information Technology" (IT for short) business has turned out to be a rather tumultuous one. Technological developments fluctuate hastily and globally; so it affects everyone involved in it. Thus, it happened with both of my sons.

They experienced layoffs and incidences with so-called "headhunters" who would inevitably lead them to new and varied job offers. It also meant pulling up geographical roots and getting transplanted to other locations.

Both Dan and Gabe Jr. underwent such happenings. Dan had to move to New Jersey to work at MaxFlight as a computer programmer. He seemed fairly content at his job, with his Cessna plane tied down at a nearby airport. He continued to fly on weekends when the weather allowed; and in fact, would often take some of his officemates flying with him.

Unbeknownst to us, Dan had fallen in love with a Russian office mate (but it was unrequited). He had bought one of those nesting Russian dolls that we had later found in his desk drawer. Dan was also trying to learn the Russian language; as he had accumulated instruction books, tapes, dictionary, and other materials. We can only speculate about his unresolved feelings and how it had affected his already failing heart!

On other weekends, Dan would visit with his older sister Lara at her home in New Jersey; and interact with his nephews and niece. They developed close ties with his new "family." In fact, he had put up a picture of Lara and her family on his desk. Often, he would ask Lara how to prepare his favorite Filipino food, "lumpia." However, he never did learn how to cook for himself, depending on fast food (to his detriment)!

We were appalled when, on one weekend, Lara telephoned us to report that Dan was in the hospital after a heart attack! He was only 30 years old!

We drove straightaway to the hospital and checked into a motel next to it. The desk clerk was astonished when we reported that we needed a room so we could go to the hospital next door to visit with our son who had just had a heart attack! Wide-eyed, he asked how old was our son? He couldn't believe it!

Thankfully, the doctors were able to insert stents into Dan's blocked heart vessels to counteract the stoppage of blood flow. It was there when we met with Dan's Office Manager who had come to visit him. The surgery was successful ad we all resumed the threads of our lives.

After this incident, Dan had become more conscious of his diet choices; and had begun to learn how to cook (coached by his sister Lara) more healthful foods. His favorite dish is the Filipino "lumpia," which is a version of the Chinese egg roll. It consists of ground pork and shrimps sautéed with plenty of vegetables; wrapped in paper-thin egg/flour wrappers and fried. It is eaten with either garlic/vinegar or sweet-sour sauce.

There was one memorable Thanksgiving when I had the incomparable joy of having had all of my children at home to celebrate with us! Lara and her family came to our house; and so did Gabe Jr. Our youngest daughter (now called "Marisol") took time off her bar-tending roles to be home with us. And Dan actually flew his plane from New Jersey to Sanford, Maine; so he could be with us! It was the most memorable Thanksgiving of my life!

We continued to make occasional visits to New Jersey to get together with all our children. It was around this time that Gabe Jr. had been laid off his job and moved in with his brother Dan at his New Jersey apartment while pursuing advanced computer studies. Simultaneously, our youngest daughter (Marisol) was working in various eating establishments with her then boyfriend, who was a chef. We managed to get the family together on special occasions.

At one time, our daughter Lara wanted to celebrate her eldest son Derek's 8th birthday by renting a beach house at Virginia Beach. We were all together, except for Dan. But on the last weekend of our rental, early one morning, I couldn't sleep, so I ventured out to the beach in front of the house.

In the distance, I saw a figure seated on a dune with his back to the house, looking at the sunrise. My heart skipped a beat, recognizing it as Dan. He had actually flown his plane from New Jersey to the closest airport in Virginia Beach!

I tiptoed along the sand to where he was seated, and gently tapped him on the shoulder, whispering his name… Dan jolted at the sound, flabbergasted! I apologized for startling him and asked when he arrived. We engaged in some small talk as I invited him back to the house.

Our family was complete again; and we will always have those memories along Virginia Beach to hold in our hearts!

DAN'S PLANE AND FAMILY

AFTERTHOUGHT

Business and industry affect all of our lives in many ways. They have local and international consequences; and individual lives are upended, elevated, or crushed by the concomitant circumstances.

It was not unusual that twins gravitated toward similar interests, even more so than just regular siblings. But they will even mimic physical motions and ailments; as well as occupations and hobbies. In fact, studies have shown how even physically-separated twins eventually exhibit identical life choices/results.

Time is immutable and needs to be considered with great care. It has been customary to say the usual "…I'll do it when I have time"…but that time never seems to come!

As already stated, there is no other time but "NOW." Now is the moment we have to live fully…

Everything else is to be relegated to the realms of memory…

Chapter 9

MOTHER'S DAY 2005

It was May of 2005 and "Mother's Day" was coming up. It was not exactly a day that I especially celebrated (except to send my Mom a carefully selected card/gift).

I went about my usual daily schedule with no particular plans. As usual after work, I pulled into our driveway to pick up the mail before going inside the house. I spied a brown package tied with a rubber band to our mailbox (since it obviously didn't fit in the box). I thought nothing of it...

Taking all the letters and the package back into the car, I halfway wondered about the package. The return address showed Dan's name and address; and my heart skipped a beat!

Still seated in the car, I tore open the brown paper to see what was inside; and it was a pencil-drawn portrait of my granddaughter Marissa! There was a small card alongside it that read: "Happy Mother's Day, mom. I thought I'd send you a portrait of everyone's favorite little girl, Marissa…love, Dan." It was signed in pencil: Dan 5/5/5.

Without hesitation, I burst into tears! I held the entire package against my heart, clutching it as I sat in the driver's seat, crying! I wept tears of mixed joy and heartache for what seemed like forever!

Time stopped, it seemed. I don't know how long I sat there, crying. Jumbled thoughts crowded in my head, together with a deep pain in my heart that, at the time, I failed to understand (but now I know it was the apprehension of doom).

Somehow, the numbers 5/5/5 shadowed portent for me… I vaguely remembered the number "5" to allegedly be the universal "lucky" number; but it did not feel lucky for me.

The overwhelming feeling was dread, which I hastily brushed aside. I automatically went about my tasks that day without a second thought.

It was around this time that Dan's company was starting to have commercial problems (about which we had no idea until after Dan's death). Sometimes they would either have reduced paychecks or no paychecks at all! We didn't find out until later that Dan was having financial difficulties as Dan was never one to complain whenever he had any money problems.

Dan's brother Gabe Jr., who now lived with him, had been taking advanced computer courses and had some savings to help out. But we had no idea that Dan was in dire straits financially. No doubt the stress must have contributed mightily to his failing heart!

So it was that, at the last week of October 2006, we received another phone call from Lara. Again, she reported that Dan had been admitted to the Medical Center with his second heart attack!

Of course we hurried to travel to Lara's house, where we could stay to monitor Dan's situation. Panic overcame my heart and spirit! It seemed my dark premonitions on Mother's Day had come to a head; and my soul sank to my feet…

My husband Tito and I drove to the Medical Center and were ushered into a hallway where we sat on a bench while we were told that the doctors would like to speak with us! DREAD overpowered me!

Shortly after, the Hospital Chaplain came to explain that Dan's heart was failing; and he requested us to come into the room where staff was working on him; so we could pray together! Crestfallen and dumbfounded, we silently followed him into the room where Dan lay while attendants worked on him.

We held one another's hands around Dan's bed as the Chaplain began to sing "On Eagle's Wings." We achingly joined in song as the pain in my heart sank to astounding proportions…

Halloween will never be the same again!…

PORTRAIT OF MARISSA

AFTERTHOUGHT

The arc of the universe trends in an unchartered course. Humans devise varied ways to try and track and interpret it. There is the use of numerology, astrology, voodoo, and other ways and means. But sadly it remains a guessing game…

It is only after an event has transpired that we glean the factors and elements that led to it. The puzzle pieces fall into place. There are those who are "wise" among us who have learned the lessons and try to teach us (who are less intuitive)…

We go to school to learn facts and figures. We learn to read and write and add and subtract etc. etc. etc. But life teaches us the hard-knock lessons. It teaches us to cope; to prepare for eventualities; to gather for future needs; to assess past events. Past and present meld into future. We are the sum total of all that we have been.

Let us be grateful for all the good we strive to do. Let us take advantage of the sacrament of the moment."

"NOW" is the only meaningful reality…

Chapter 10

HEART TRANSPLANT

Since the Medical Center where Dan was situated did not have the resources or infrastructure for a heart transplant, the staff decided to have him transported by ambulance to the nearest facility that did, i.e. Newark Beth-Israel Hospital in Newark, New Jersey. We were instructed to follow the ambulance to that hospital.

As it happened, on the final leg of the journey in the ambulance, Dan "flat lined" as they were approaching the emergency entrance. As he was being unloaded, three cardiologists (who were just there by happenstance) met the gurney and started to revive him.

Later on, someone remarked that it was like Dan's guardian angel was right there by his side, working overtime to supervise the event. The emergency room staff immediately sprung into action to facilitate Dan's recovery. They managed to get the consent of the patient who was supposed to be next in line at the ER to allow Dan's emergency surgery to be done right away (before their turn). Time was of the essence! All the pieces came together and Dan was able to be resuscitated and stabilized enough to be transferred to the CCU unit.

The waiting was intolerable! We, the family members of the two patients being treated, were cramped into a small waiting room turned into a makeshift campsite. An assortment of pillows and blankets were furnished by the staff for our long wait. The other patient's family (who had so graciously allowed Dan's treatment to pre-empt their mother's case) had come prepared with containers of hot food. On the other hand, we were too stressed out to either eat or sleep…

Because we (as the family) were from out of state, the hospital was gracious enough to allow us free lodging while our loved one was hospitalized. We were accorded spacious quarters in a furnished apartment with living-dining-kitchen facilities; as well as a bedroom and bath! This way, we could keep track of Dan instantaneously!

Meanwhile, Tito and I had to deal with our job situations. He was fortunate enough to have a big-hearted boss who assured him that everything would be adjusted to suit his needs. (He would not lose his job.) I, on the other hand, had to rely on my co-workers' donating their sick/vacation hours to me (otherwise I had no work - no pay)! It really did not matter to me, as it was a question of Dan's life or death! Earning money was the last thing on my mind!!!

The month of November was like a roller coaster of events. As we awakened in the morning, I would go down to the cafeteria to get breakfast items that I would bring back to the apartment. We'd visit with Dan who was always glad to see us. Often, members of our family would also come to visit. There was my brother-in-law Jake and his wife Mila from New Jersey; as well as my sister Cora and her family; and my brother Don and his wife Pat. There was also my brother Mon and his wife Vicky from Virginia; as well as my sister Angela and her husband Rey. My cousin Red's wife Sol (who worked as a nurse in the hospital) would often bring food and check in on us. My other cousin Freddie (who is an internist), together with his wife Vivien (also an internist), made regular calls to check in on Dan's status. Freddie's sister, Olive, also kept vigil with me for a whole day.

Of course, there were my daughter Lara and her family; as well as my youngest daughter Marisol (who often massaged Dan's legs and arms) who were regular visitors. Needless to say, Dan's twin brother Gabe was constantly there for him. We had a strong spiritual bond that seemed tighter than ever!

If weather permitted, Tito would return to Maine to pick up fresh clothes and check our mail. I stayed with Dan constantly; to the extent that, eventually, I did lose my job! It barely mattered to me, as all that I cared for was that Dan would get better…

As for our regular meals, it would have cost us a fortune were we to eat three times a day at the cafeteria. As it happened, my very generous cousins took it upon themselves to "deliver" home-cooked meals every day to us— complete with rice, condiments, sauces, etc. etc.etc! My cousins Eleanor and Red (sister and brother) arrived at early noon each day with their bounty! It warmed my heart to know I have such thoughtful family members!

There was also a special room at the hospital—a lengthy room nicely furnished with a kitchenette (full refrigerator and microwave), dining room table and chairs; sofa and easy chairs; book cases; TV and a computer. The room was locked and available only to families while a loved one was undergoing or recuperating from transplant surgery. The room had been donated to the hospital, grant-funded by a family of a former patient. The head nurse gave us the key to use the room and we were glad for the comfort and privacy!

However, a massage therapist took it upon himself to co-opt the room for his use at odd hours of the night (prompting us to question his ultimate motives for use of the room). I was urged by my cousin Red to write a letter of complaint to the president of the hospital! I did so; and the therapist was banned from further use of the room!

Thanksgiving came and went and we continued to keep vigil with Dan. Since the hospital was non denominational, they had a designated "prayer room" decorated with stained glass, benches, and greenery. I would often go there and meditate and pray. I noticed Islamist individuals whose bodies were bent in prayer, kissing the ground. There were people fingering beads or pounding their chests. I closed my eyes to concentrate on my petitions. All of a sudden, I felt a touch on my shoulder. I looked up to see a woman staring down at me. She asked, "Do you have someone in the hospital to be praying for?" I replied, "My son." Without any hesitation, she stated, "He will be revived and live a long life. Do not fear!" then turned to leave me, with my mouth agape! But my heart was uplifted!

It was similar to an epiphany moment I had one moonlit November night at the apartment. I was saying my evening prayers as I meditated on the full moon outside the bedroom window. Tears streamed down my face as I spoke to the Blessed Mother:"You are a mother as am I...You know how my heart is burdened by the plight of my son! Surely you realize what pain I feel, as you did yourself while your son suffered and died— please help me, help my son...Help him to get a new heart!"

As I looked back into the night sky, I was startled to see a shooting star speed from one side of the moon to the other! And a voice in my head clearly stated, "Don't worry. On my Immaculate Conception, Dan will get a new heart..."

Both shock and awe overcame me! Could it be true? I dared not hope but could not escape the shuddering feelings!

It doesn't take much to lift or dampen one's spirits. I had almost gotten used to the roller-coaster rhythm of life in the hospital. November was almost over; going into our second month in the hospital with Dan. We had begun to harbor some delusions of his recovery, i.e. our sale of our house in Maine while I'd rent an apartment in New Jersey to take care of Dan until his complete recovery while simultaneously resolving all the loose ends!

Sadly, we were constantly crushed by the reality of Dan's crisis each time he started bleeding and had to be rushed to the Cath Lab! At one point, we had to drive to the nearby Bank of America branch to sign papers for refinancing our house. Gabe offered to babysit his brother while we drove to the bank for a couple of hours. We had barely left the hospital parking lot when Gabe nervously telephoned that Dan had burst a blood vessel and was rushed to the Cath Lab again! We hastily turned around and hurried back to the hospital…

Since that incident, we dared not leave Dan's bedside for any reason.

However, I had joined a clinical "dry-eyes" trial the previous year that necessitated regular eye appointments and testing at a New Hampshire facility. If you completed all the requirements, you would get paid $700.00. I needed only one more appointment on December 6th and so I decided to take just 3 days off (including 2 days' travel time to and from Maine) while Tito would stay in New Jersey with Dan. In the back of my mind was Our Lady's promise that Dan would get a new heart by the feast of her Immaculate Conception (December 8). I was convinced that it would happen. As fate would have it, a phone call from Tito reported that a car accident victim's heart was becoming available to transplant to Dan!

Happily, the weather cooperated and I could drive back from Maine on December 7th. With an eager heart, I completed my appointment and testing, while taking care of laundry and mail. By the eve of December 7th, I was ready to return to the hospital in New Jersey. Then it started to rain… I prayed to the rhythm of the windshield wipers swinging back and forth: "O Mother, ever help us…"

True to form, the darkness of night—the rain—the odd rhythm of the windshield wipers—all combined to make me lose what little sense of direction I had!

Very nervous and visibly stressed, I stopped at a well-lit Diner, where I tearfully pleaded with the staff how my son was scheduled for a heart transplant right about that time at the nearby Medical Center, but I couldn't find my way there! They were moved at my plight and managed to write down specific instructions on how to get back on the right track.

I still don't know how I managed, but eventually I recognized familiar landmarks and finally found my way to the hospital. Dan was tearfully desperate to see me…we hugged…in the midst of my tears as he nervously prepared to undergo his heart transplant surgery…

Our Holy Mother had kept her promise—a new heart was transplanted into my son on her Immaculate Conception!

AFTERTHOUGHTS

Keeping vigil is a practice honored in many cultures and religions. The use of fire (as in candles and torches) has a separate utility when included in ceremonies.

For example, the death of a person is clothed in various types of practices. Christians usually hold a "wake," or keeping vigil in a funeral parlor with the casket holding the deceased, surrounded by the grieving loved ones. Flowers and songs abound; as do elegies and testimonials about the departed one. Ministers and pastors often perform ceremonial rites.

In many native, primitive cultures, lively songs and dances are performed with wild movements and colorful costumes. Chants and monologues are intoned or spoken, and burnt offerings made.

The Jews sit "shiva," or gatherings in the home of the deceased, where reminiscences of him/her are narrated, and food offerings given.

Universally, the life of a person is celebrated in one way or another to mark its passage from the temporal to the eternal. Life is fleeting, no matter how long or short it is. What is important is that it remain significant, no matter what!

Omens play a separate, significant role in momentous events of life and/or death. Religious beliefs and practices hold great sway over the meaning attributed to an omen or a prediction offered by a person or a group. When it comes to pass, it can be overwhelming!

In the Christian tradition, it can be called a "miracle" when it transcends physical boundaries. Regardless of faith or culture, however, humans tend to recognize when something out of the natural realm occurs…

Chapter 11

THE LONG GOODBYE

There is a magical shadow around the number "3" in history, in theology, as well as in practical reality. We are all aware of the three-leaf clover and the three persons of the Holy Trinity; and most people agree that "the third time is the charm." But when we find ourselves confronted by everyday happenings that happen to occur during the 3rd hour of the 3rd day of the week for 3 weeks in a row, it starts to defy the notion of coincidence!

It all started in late December of 2006, on a Wednesday (the 3rd day of the week) at around 3 o'clock in the afternoon during one of our daily vigils at Dan's bedside. The nurse informed us that a blood vessel had burst and he was being brought to the Cath Lab for remedial procedures.

After Dan's transplant, the heart that he was given from the female victim of a car accident was pumping very well in his chest. Unfortunately, all of the open-heart procedures to which he had constantly been subjected, had stripped his chest area wide open to multiple virulent organisms that managed to invade the surrounding tissues, cells and blood vessels that were exposed time and time again to widespread infection. This not only impaired his overall condition but also subdued the standard functioning of his regular organs. Dan was weakening substantially.

To stem the tide, the medical staff went into overdrive to conduct a heroic research program to try and identify new protocols (even the latest medications that had not yet been approved by the FDA) and experimental methods that they could utilize to counteract Dan's infection. His lead doctor, Dr. Mendoza, was extremely conscientious in her research. They tried every alternative possible. But everything seemed so futile…

In my heart of hearts, I had to confront the reality that I would lose my son…I was shattered into a million pieces! When he was finally brought back to his room after the Cath Lab procedure, I sat by his bedside and held his hand silently. I stroked his arm and his face as I smiled tenderly and reassuringly at him. We were in wordless communion (except with our eyes, by which we exchanged tons of love). In my mind swirled millions of words that I could have uttered but I swallowed them painfully as the thoughts flew swiftly from my mind to his…somehow I knew he knew! We communicated internally…

I was reminded of a similar incident years ago, when my Dad was in the hospital the day before he died. Dad and I were together briefly as he lay in his bed, gazing silently into my eyes. I gazed back at him, outpouring gazillions of tons of love to him through my eyes. I sensed that he received it, just as Dan was receiving my love offering at this very moment. Saying goodbye to two men in my life whom I loved so deeply was so equally painful in its silent tension!

It so happened that the trips to the Cath Lab transpired for 3 weeks in a row, at around the same time in the afternoon. I was not the only one who noticed the pattern—the nurses did, too.

Later on, I surmised that it was such a roundabout way to say goodbye; like dragging one's feet to prolong the finality of a dreaded occurrence. The instinct for survival is so strong in every being that, in the face of impending death, there remains the desire to remain in the land of the living!

On one of those trips to the Cath Lab, Dan was uncharacteristically communicative. With trembling fingers, he wrote in shaky letters that he wanted to make his Last Will and Testament. Frozen inside, I did not hesitate to respond by rushing to the hospital's clerical staff to assist in the matter. But since it was a federal holiday in January (Martin Luther King Day), there was nobody on staff to do it!

However, because it was a holiday, Dan's siblings were all present and wanting to be with him, ministering to his needs. Marisol was busy massaging his arms and legs. Lara was trying to find a way to get the kids permission to visit their Uncle Dan. Other friends and relatives were waiting in the wings.

Gabe Jr. was particularly engrossed in communication with his twin. He copied parts of the "Patient's Bill of Rights" that was prominently hanging on a wall; as he conferred its particulars with his brother. I'm sure he constantly conveyed his deep love for Dan!

My heart sank, as I realized that Dan was painfully aware that his end was coming. Although we had been with him all day (even skipping lunch), I did not feel like leaving him. But the nurse came in to remind him that he needed to return to the Cath Lab. Even Dan was hesitant, as he motioned with his fingers for us to stay with him (subconsciously aware that we did not have any moments to spare being together).

But my logical mind overruled my aching heart, as I assured Dan that we would see him again, and that we loved him very much. Little did I realize that those would be my last words to him.

We had not had anything to eat since breakfast and the physical stress was starting to take its toll. Hesitant though I was, it was imperative for us to say goodbye until the next day. We stayed standing at the doorway of Dan's room as they wheeled him away to the Cath Lab. Our last view of Dan was his wasted thin arm weakly raised high waving his last goodbye. It remains indelible in our hearts!

The sight of Dan's outstretched arm tremblingly waving goodbye was like a sword that pierced our souls standing by the hallway that night.

Back in the apartment, Tito and were both starting to relax after dinner when the phone rang. The nurse's voice broke in a tremor: "Dan is in trouble…" Without wanting to hear any more, I flung into action — grabbed the apartment keys; put a vial of holy oil in my jacket pocket; hurriedly muttered something to Tito about Dan, and flew out of the apartment as fast as I could, with Tito at my heels…

Thinking back to that flight from our apartment in one wing of the hospital to Dan's room in a separate wing at the CCU, it's all a blur in my mind. All I know is that I had never walked so fast and furious in my life!

By the time I reached the floor to Dan's room, attendants were shuttering the hallway so no one could enter as I shouted, "He's my son! I need to see my son!" Someone gently put their arms around me as I was ushered away, stating that the emergency crew was working to revive Dan and could not be hindered in any way. I was tearful and unwilling to be held back… forcefully shoved into the tiny prayer room by the attendants; where I finally, hopelessly, dropped on my knees onto the cold tile floor, with my arms flung in prayer, uttering the Hail Mary in between sobs…

As I reached the words"…now and at the hour of our death…" I felt a distinct shudder around my entire upper torso—a shudder like I have never, ever felt before (or since)—which made me stop shakily, totally unnerved! A few seconds later, a nurse opened the door to inform us that Dan had died! Somehow, I already knew…

The shudder that electrified me as I was praying felt like every nerve in my being was vibrating at supersonic speed in electromagnetic fashion, bristling my very core in a blinding fury such as I had never before (or ever again) experienced. It was like Dan's spirit enveloped me in a metaphysical embrace of atoms shivering and intermingling electronically. It was a supersonic goodbye!

That night, in the apartment, I moaned and wailed like a wounded animal, crying wordlessly in the bedroom, punching my pillow—I felt past any and all consolation…a night to end all nights!

AFTERTHOUGHT

Life and death = the two pillars at each end of one's tombstone. Life is represented by a short dash between two numbers: the date of birth, and the date of death. How ironic that each of our lives is only a short dash between two dates! That's all there is to it, no matter how long or short the life; no matter how meaningful or not…

All the events that transpired; the relationships that ebbed and flowed; acts of stupidity and/or heroism that were manifested; etc. etc.—are covered in that little dash. Prominent people receive substantial elegies; the unknown, regular people (or dregs of humanity) receive little or no recognition. Such is human life!

Death, on the other hand, is often marked or remembered, depending on the details involved. Armed conflicts (like wars) or natural disasters (like storms, fires, and earthquakes) result in memorable victims. So do murders or vehicular accidents. But also deaths due to unusual circumstances usually merit distinctive notice. This includes extraordinary medical cases or deaths from which unforgettable significance occurs.

For example, if a circle of life is completed by the event of a death… when something or somebody emerges as the seeming fruit of the process…it becomes significant!

Such was Dan's passing…

THE "NEW" DANIEL WITH HIS "LOLO"

Chapter 12

THE CIRCLE OF LIFE

Grief is an individual experience. It is usually accompanied by a state of shock after a terrible event. My daughter Lara and her family took us into their home after Dan's death; since we had to vacate the hospital apartment. Our other daughter Marisol and her boyfriend Jason helped us to clear out the place. The whole experience felt like sleepwalking. We could not eat; or sleep; or even cry. We were dumbfounded, going through the motions of planning for the funeral.

Lara's husband Nelson's cousin (Father Ed) was a parish priest at the nearby Cabrini Catholic Church and provided us with great spiritual support. He helped us with the funeral mass and last rites arrangements. Significant emotional and financial support emerged from family and friends. It served as a welcome balm to our cocoon of stinging grief. But it could not serve to open up the dam of tears embedded in my soul. I remained tearlessly stoic in my state of shock.

There was, in the midst of my darkness, a ray of light. I did have the solace of being able to bare my heart to Nancy, my spiritual director, who had been in constant contact with me by telephone over the course of Dan's hospital stay. After I reported how Dan had passed away, she always seemed to be able to find the right words to soothe me—a tender balm for my soul wounds! I also received reassuring phone calls from other friends: my long-time friend Lori-Ann, as well as a couple of friends from Maine (Lucy and Pam); as well as my prayer group leader Mary.

Amazingly, I functioned with flawless efficiency attending to the minutiae of the funeral. I met and discussed details with the funeral director; arranged and paid for the burial plots; contracted with the infrastructure for the reception and food, flowers, etc. etc. No stone was left unturned. It was almost like I needed to exert myself straight out like a rubber band stretched to its limit; so as to disallow the slightest sliver of pain to filter through the bedlam.

During the wake, my sisters and family members provided refreshments at the funeral home; and helped entertain the numerous friends and relatives who were in attendance… It was a refreshing surprise to meet a group of Dan's cousins (for the first time) who had flown in from Chicago to commiserate his passing. They represented four relatives on the Dela Rosa side of the family whom we met for the first time. They had received the news on the internet and decided to fly to New Jersey to attend his funeral. One of them remarked on how Dan's musical talent (which I had noted when I narrated how Dan had taught himself to play both the guitar and the violin) was a reflection of an uncle who had been famous during his time for his virtuoso in playing the violin! Who knew?!?!?

A delegation of co-workers from Dan's office (including his boss) was also present. Frank, the boss, could not get over the physical resemblance of Gabe Jr. to his twin brother Dan! He also stated how he had instructed the office personnel who had been clamoring to visit Dan while he was in the hospital to refrain from physical proximity, in order to avoid infection (which did turn out to be his doom).

A close friend of Dan's at work, named John, confided that he had very much wanted to come and visit Dan but was repeatedly assailed by the boss. John revealed that he and Dan had had long discussions and detailed conversations over the years on any and all manner of subjects. He added how insightful and deep were their talks, which he would truly miss!

It struck a chord in my memory of an instance when Dan was happy to try and communicate via the internet on his brother's laptop. But since he could not speak due to being intubated; we devised a method of communication using the alphabet to spell out his answers to our questions. Unfortunately, we hit an impasse in the process when we came to spelling out the friend's last name; i.e. we figured out that his first initial was "J" but failed to decipher the rest of it (in order to complete the email address). In hindsight, at the funeral, it dawned on me that the "J" stood for "John," who was the one Dan wanted desperately to contact! It was simply one of the loose ends that had to be straightened out…

There were other loose ends that pertained to Dan's belongings. Lara and Marisol helped Gabe Jr. negotiate the termination of his apartment lease. We also managed to return his car to the dealer; and emptied out his apartment of its contents. Driving to his office, we cleaned out his desk of his personal belongings (which included a set of nesting Russian dolls; Russian dictionary and phonetics books; bird feeder parts; stationery and pictures). It was very sobering…

Six weeks after his funeral, my heart literally broke! I had a heart attack which necessitated angioplasty to insert a couple of stents to repair my blocked heart vessels. The stress of the last few months had resulted in the actual, physical tearing apart of my heart… Only the soothing, warming love of my family and friends rescued me!

Resilience is a life line when hooked up to the strong bond of family love and togetherness. We struggled and leaned upon one another in our desperate attempt to traverse the lengthy, uphill climb towards a sense of normalcy.

Gabe Jr. had the worst of it, since he was the other half of a twinship; and that other physical half was gone! I could only imagine his pain; but, unbeknownst to us, he was moving in a positive direction!

Gabe had joined an online dating service, through which he had met several Filipino girls. He had even gone on a trip to the Philippines to meet with a couple of them! In returning to the roots of his ethnicity, Gabe was learning some very basic facets of his personality. He was coming face to face with his essence—and it was helping to heal him!

As it happened, he returned to New Jersey; got a new job; and met and fell in love with Cecille, a Filipino accountant who lived and worked in New York.

In short order, our families met and they were engaged. Their wedding was held in the Philippines, where her mother lives; after which they returned to New Jersey.

Today, Gabe and Cecille have bought a house in New Jersey, where they live with their little son, named Daniel (after his departed uncle). The boy was born prematurely after IVF treatments; and has become the love of our lives…

The circle of life is now completed with the coming of the new Daniel!

FINAL AFTERTHOUGHT

Life is a circle—with a starting point, curving outwards to its ultimate ending point—interspersed with countless who's, what's, where's, when's and how's; and motivated by numerous why's…

The intervening distances between those two points can be as brief as being instantaneous; or as lengthy as being over a hundred years. No one ever truly knows! It has been given names such as "fate" or "destiny" or "karma" or even posited as "reincarnation" by some.

Culture (and Nature) do color that space in between. Character and habits are formulated by the events, relationships, inherited genes and outward influences that the person experiences. It is the greatest mystery!

When we are born, we embark on the most profound journey of all… As a toddler, we are amazed by the smoothness and greenness of a blade of grass—the impact of which is lost to the adult caregiver! Similar juxtapositions occur as we grow older… The novelty and beauty of nature starts to fade into ordinariness! Such a pity!

We must never lose that sense of mystery! Unfortunately, we have to suffer the jolt of some intense tragedy to catapult us into this realization. Sometimes, it is the unexpected death of a beloved child that acts as a lightning bolt from the universe. It has been said that the death of a child is the most painful by its very nature… Parents do not bury children—it's supposed to be the other way around!

The birth of the new Daniel has become a sort of atonement…as though the universe, in its painful attempt to recompense the sudden snatching of the first Daniel, has made amends for its tragic deed.

Life is a question. Life is a mystery. The answer will only be known on the other side…

***

GABRIEL, THE "NEW" DANIEL & CECILE

www.ingramcontent.com/pod-product-compliance
Lightning Source LLC
Chambersburg PA
CBHW081757100526
44592CB00015B/2469